Food Field Trips

Let's Explore
Apples!

Jill Colella

Lerner Publications ◆ Minneapolis

Hello, Friends,

Everybody eats, even from birth. This is why learning about food is important. Making the right choices about what to eat begins with knowing more about food. Food literacy helps us be curious about food and adventurous about what we eat. In short, it helps us discover how delicious the world of food can be.

I enjoy picking ripe apples. I take the apples inside, wash them off, and decide how to eat them. How do you like to eat your apples? I love dipping apple slices in peanut butter.

For more inspiration, ideas, and recipes, visit www.teachkidstocook.com.

Jill

About the Author

Happy cook, reformed picky eater, and longtime classroom teacher Jill Colella founded both *Ingredient* and *Butternut*, award-winning children's magazines that promote food literacy.

Lerner Publications Company
An imprint of Lerner Publishing Group, Inc.
241 First Avenue North
Minneapolis, MN 55401 USA

For reading levels and more information, look up this title at www.lernerbooks.com.

Main body text set in Mikado. Typeface provided by HVD.

Library of Congress Cataloging-in-Publication Data

Names: Colella, Jill, author.
Title: Let's explore apples! / by Jill Colella.
Description: Minneapolis : Lerner Publications, [2020] | Series: Food field
   trips | Includes bibliographical references and index. |
   Audience: Age 4–8. | Audience: K to Grade 3.
Identifiers: LCCN 2019011160 (print) | LCCN
   2019014590 (ebook) | ISBN 9781541581784 (eb pdf) |
   ISBN 9781541563001 (lb : alk. paper)
Subjects: LCSH: Apple—Juvenile literature.
Classification: LCC SB363 (ebook) | LCC SB363 .C65 2020
   (print) | DDC 634/.11—dc23

LC record available at https://lccn.loc.gov/2019011160

Manufactured in the United States of America
3-52577-47539-2/10/2022

SCAN FOR BONUS CONTENT!

Table of Contents

Picture Glossary

apple tree

core

half

mash

orchard

ALL ABOUT APPLES

Apples are firm and crunchy. You can eat them in many ways.

You can take a bite from an unpeeled apple. You can cut an apple into slices and dip them in peanut butter or caramel.

Cooked apples are soft and delicious. Apples can be baked into yummy foods such as pies or doughnuts.

Apples are juicy. Squeezed apples make apple juice!

LET'S COMPARE

Apples come in many shapes, sizes, colors, and even tastes. Some taste sweet, and some taste tart.

Granny Smith apples are tart and green.

Honeycrisp apples are sweet.

McIntosh apples are juicy.

What kind of apples do you like best?

LET'S EXPLORE

The apple at the top is a whole apple. The apple below it is cut in half.

Look at the half. Do you see the core? Do you spot the seeds? Can you find the surprise?

Inside the apple is a special surprise shape. A star! A star has as many points as an apple tree flower has petals. Count them!

LET'S GO PICK APPLES

Apples grow on trees. An orchard is a fruit tree farm.

Visiting an orchard is lots of fun.
You can pick your own fruits
right from a tree. Let's go pick
some apples!

There are apples down low.
There are apples up high.

There are big apples and small apples. There are apples hanging from the trees. There are apples on the ground.

What kind of trees are in an apple orchard?

There is an apple way up high.
We can't reach it!

Ask an adult for help. An adult can lift you so you can reach the apple. If it's still too high, the adult can help you use a ladder.

We need lots of apples to make applesauce.

Do you think we have enough apples? How many apples can you count?

We must fill the basket with apples.
Is the basket full yet?

Animals like apples too!

What animals might you see in an apple tree?

Look at the apples we picked! We have big apples, small apples, and medium-sized apples!

LET'S COOK

Try these varieties for great applesauce: Granny Smith, Rome Beauty, Fuji, and Jonagold. Always have an adult present when working in the kitchen!

APPLESAUCE

INGREDIENTS

- 4 apples
- ¾ cup (177 ml) water
- 1 tablespoon brown sugar
- ½ teaspoon ground cinnamon

1. Peel, core, and dice the apples.

2. Put diced apples, water, brown sugar, and cinnamon in a medium saucepan and stir.

peel

core

chop

3. Cover saucepan and place over medium heat.

4. Cook for 15 to 20 minutes or until apples are soft.

5. Remove from heat, and allow apples to cool.

6. Using a masher, mash the mixture until your applesauce is as chunky or smooth as you like it. Makes 4 servings.

SEE THIS RECIPE IN ACTION!

LET'S TASTE

Try having an apple-tasting party! Gather a variety of apples. Try a slice of each.

Pay attention to the taste, texture, and scent. Have everyone vote for a favorite apple. Use a sheet of paper to keep track of everyone's favorite. See which apple wins!

Here are some varieties you might try:

Baldwin

Cortland

Crispin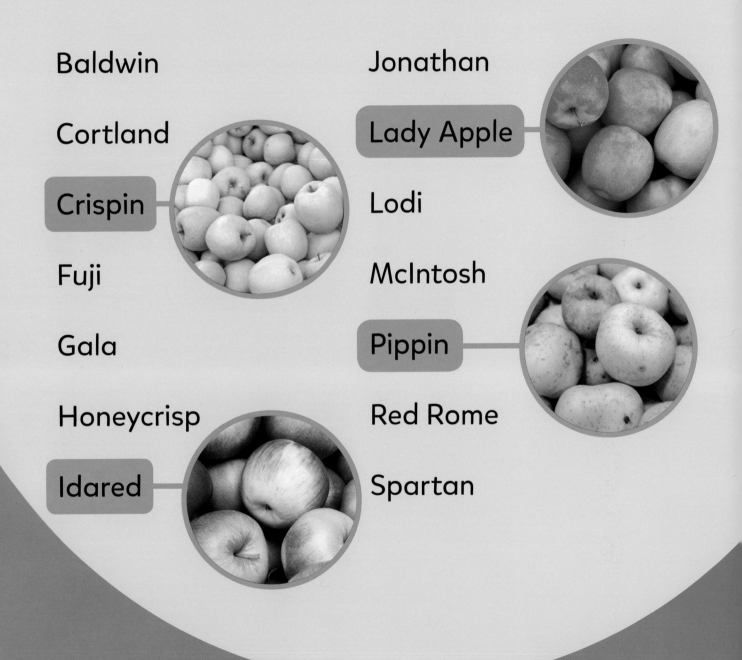

Fuji

Gala

Honeycrisp

Idared

Jonathan

Lady Apple

Lodi

McIntosh

Pippin

Red Rome

Spartan

Let's Read

Apples for Education
http://apples4ed.com

Clark, Rosalyn. *A Visit to the Orchard*. Minneapolis: Lerner Publications, 2018.

Rustad, Martha E. H. *Fall Apple Fun*. Minneapolis: Lerner Publications, 2019.

US Apples
http://usapple.org

Index

Photo Acknowledgments

Image credits: blueeyes/Shutterstock.com, pp. 1, 23 (lady apple); imagenavi/Getty Images, p. 3 (half); ranplett/Getty Images, p. 3 (core); Johner Images/Getty Images, p. 3 (tree); annick vanderschelden photography/Getty Images, p. 3 (mashed); images72/Shutterstock.com, p. 3 (orchard); cometary/Getty Images, p. 4; Suzanne Tucker/Getty Images, p. 5 (doughnuts); JGI/Jamie Grill/Getty Images, p. 5 (juice); Lesyy/Getty Images, p. 5 (pie); Darios/Shutterstock.com, p. 6; wholden/Getty Images, p. 7 (Honeycrisp); Thn Rocn Khosit Rath Phachr Sukh/EyeEm/Getty Images, p. 7 (Granny Smith); Jeff Thrower/Shutterstock.com, p. 7 (McIntosh); Rosmarie Wirz/Moment/Getty Images, p. 8 (top); Nazzu/Shutterstock.com, p. 8 (bottom); Annalisa Manzo/EyeEm/Getty Images, p. 9 (flower); Laura Westlund/Independent Picture Service, pp. 9, 20 (illustrations); DHuss/Getty Images, p. 10 (baskets); Cavan Images/Getty Images, pp. 10 (picking apple), 15; RomrodphotoShutterstock.com, p. 10 (boys); FamVeld/Shutterstock.com, p. 11; susan.k./Getty Images, pp. 12, 16 (girl); sarahdoow/Getty Images, p. 12 (branch); Deb Perry/Getty Images, p. 13; Onfokus/Getty Images, p. 14; phototropic/iStock/Getty Images, p. 16 (boy); Lubos Chlubny/Shutterstock.com, p. 17; Mordolff/Getty Images, p. 18 (caterpillar); Photos by By Deb Alperin/Getty Images, p. 18 (bee); Nataba/Getty Images, p. 18 (bird); Moving Moment/Shutterstock.com, p. 19; bhofack2/Getty Images, p. 20 (applesauce); Radius Images/Getty Images, p. 21; Jose Luis Pelaez Inc/Getty Images, p. 22; BruceBlock/E+/Getty Images, p. 23 (Crispin); gilaxia/Getty Images, p. 23 (Idared); PhotoJIGS/Shutterstock.com, p. 23 (Pippin).

Cover: John Block/Getty Images, (cider); phototropic/Getty Images, (collecting apples); Gajus/Shutterstock.com (picking apples); DebraH/Shutterstock.com, (kid); Douglas Sacha/Getty Images, (back).